Comprehensive Guitar Note Reading Guide Volume 1

MB22113

By William Bay

© 2010 BY MEL BAY PUBLICATIONS, INC., PACIFIC, MO 63069.
ALL RIGHTS RESERVED. INTERNATIONAL COPYRIGHT SECURED. B.M.I. MADE AND PRINTED IN U.S.A.
No part of this publication may be reproduced in whole or in part, or stored in a retrieval system, or transmitted in any form
or by any means, electronic, mechanical, photocopy, recording, or otherwise, without written permission of the publisher.

Visit us on the Web at www.melbay.com or www.billsmusicshelf.com

Tuning the Guitar

The six open strings of the guitar will be of the same pitch as the six notes shown in the illustration of the piano keyboard. Note that five of the strings are below the middle C of the piano keyboard.

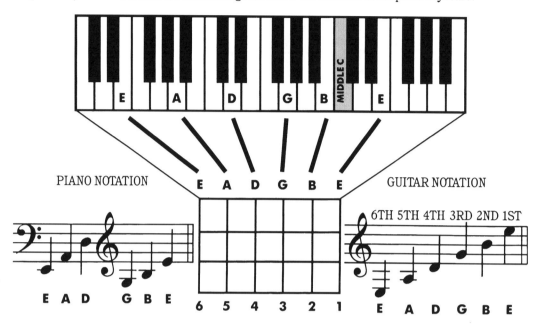

Another Method of Tuning

1. Tune the 6th string in unison with the **E** or 12th white key to the LEFT of MIDDLE C on the piano.

2. Place the finger behind the fifth fret of the 6th string. This will give you the tone or pitch of the 5th string **(A)**.

3. Place finger behind the fifth fret of the 5th string to get the pitch of the 4th string **(D)**.

4. Repeat same procedure to obtain the pitch of the 3rd string **(G)**.

5. Place finger behind the fourth fret of the 3rd string to get the pitch of the 2nd string **(B)**.

6. Place finger behind the fifth fret of the 2nd string to get the pitch of the 1st string **(E)**.

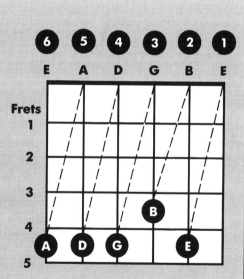

Electronic Guitar Tuner

Electronic Guitar Tuners are available at your music store. They are a handy device and highly recommended.

The Rudiments of Music

The Staff:

Music is written on a STAFF consisting of FIVE LINES and FOUR SPACES. The lines and spaces are numbered upward as shown:

```
5TH LINE ─────────────────────────
                                    4TH SPACE
4TH LINE ─────────────────────────
                                    3RD SPACE
3RD LINE ─────────────────────────
                                    2ND SPACE
2ND LINE ─────────────────────────
                                    1ST SPACE
1ST LINE ─────────────────────────
```

The lines and spaces are named after letters of the alphabet.

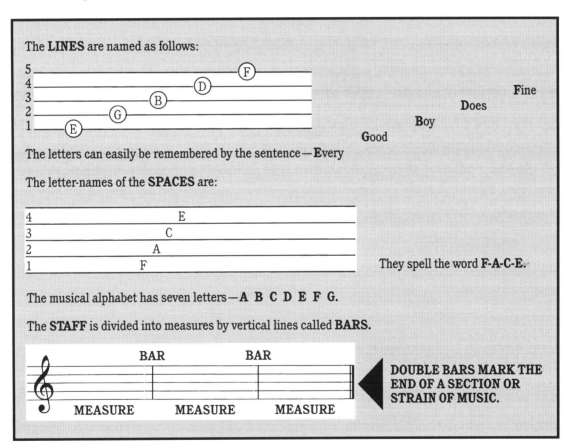

The **LINES** are named as follows:

The letters can easily be remembered by the sentence—**Every Good Boy Does Fine**

The letter-names of the **SPACES** are:

They spell the word **F-A-C-E**.

The musical alphabet has seven letters—**A B C D E F G**.

The **STAFF** is divided into measures by vertical lines called **BARS**.

DOUBLE BARS MARK THE END OF A SECTION OR STRAIN OF MUSIC.

The Clef:

This sign is the treble or G clef.

All guitar music will be written in this clef.

The second line of the treble clef is known as the G line. Many people call the treble clef the G clef because it circles around the G line.

NOTES

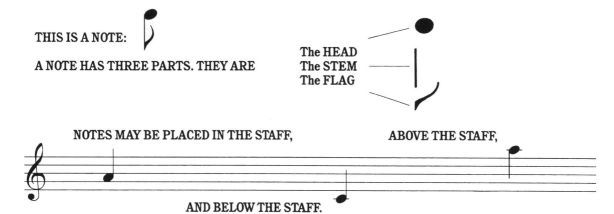

THIS IS A NOTE:

A NOTE HAS THREE PARTS. THEY ARE
- The HEAD
- The STEM
- The FLAG

NOTES MAY BE PLACED IN THE STAFF, ABOVE THE STAFF, AND BELOW THE STAFF.

A note will bear the name of the line or space it occupies on the staff.
The location of a note in, above, or below the staff will indicate the pitch.

PITCH: the height or depth of a tone.
TONE: a musical sound.

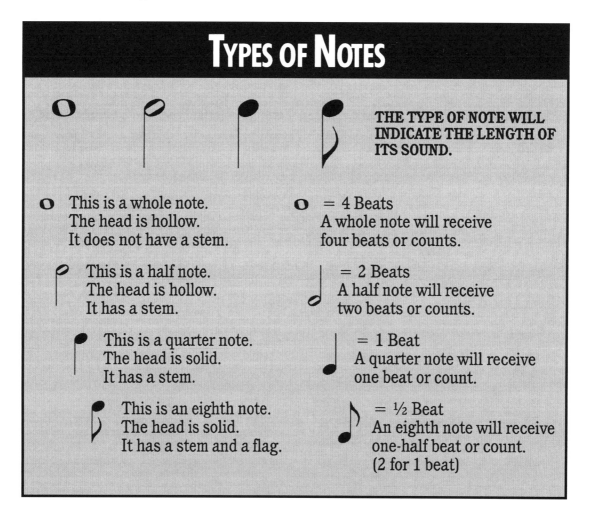

TYPES OF NOTES

THE TYPE OF NOTE WILL INDICATE THE LENGTH OF ITS SOUND.

o This is a whole note.
The head is hollow.
It does not have a stem.

o = 4 Beats
A whole note will receive four beats or counts.

This is a half note.
The head is hollow.
It has a stem.

= 2 Beats
A half note will receive two beats or counts.

This is a quarter note.
The head is solid.
It has a stem.

= 1 Beat
A quarter note will receive one beat or count.

This is an eighth note.
The head is solid.
It has a stem and a flag.

= ½ Beat
An eighth note will receive one-half beat or count.
(2 for 1 beat)

RESTS

A REST is a sign used to designate a period of silence. This period of silence will be of the same duration of time as the note to which it corresponds.

 This is an eighth rest.   This is a quarter rest.

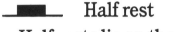 Half rest
Half rests lie on the line.

 Whole rest
Whole rests hang down from the line.

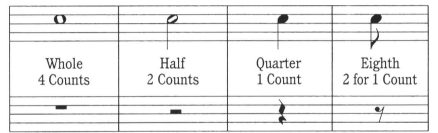

THE TIME SIGNATURE

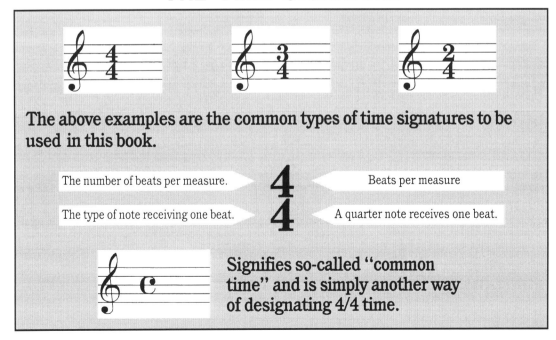

Notes on the High E String

First String

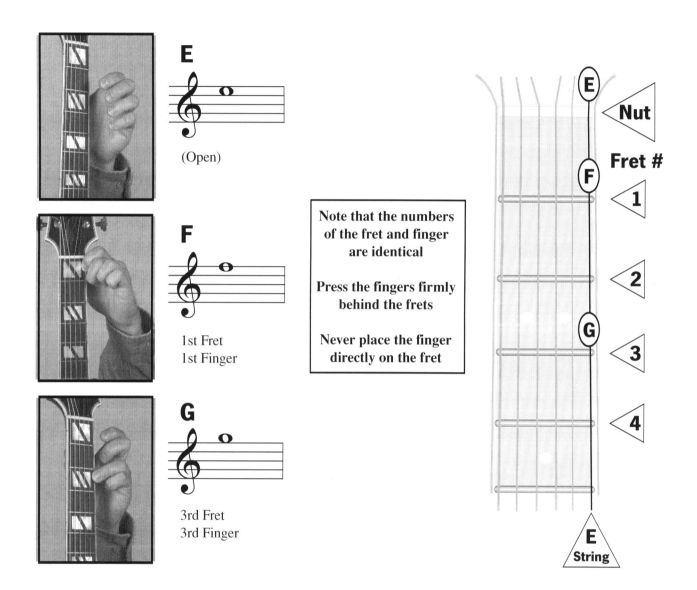

E
(Open)

F
1st Fret
1st Finger

G
3rd Fret
3rd Finger

Note that the numbers of the fret and finger are identical

Press the fingers firmly behind the frets

Never place the finger directly on the fret

Playing the Notes

Playing the Notes

Working the Fingers

1st-String Etude

Etude No. 2

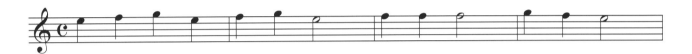

The Mixmaster

Notes on the First String
(Fill in the blocks)

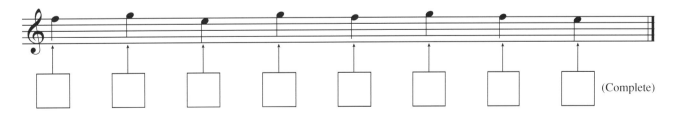

(Complete)

Notes on the B String

Second String

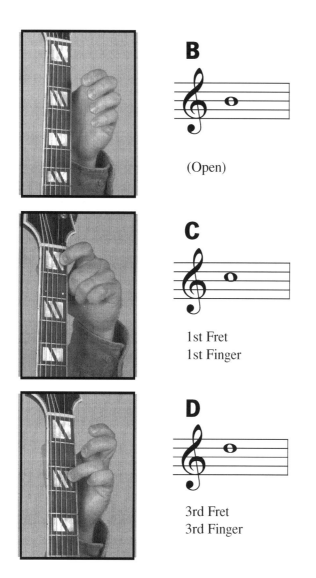

B

(Open)

C

1st Fret
1st Finger

D

3rd Fret
3rd Finger

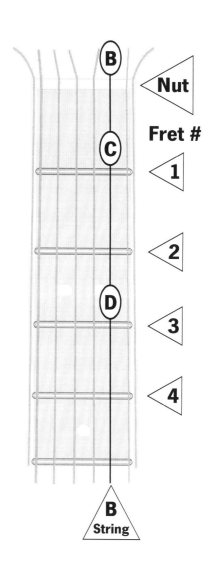

Playing the Notes

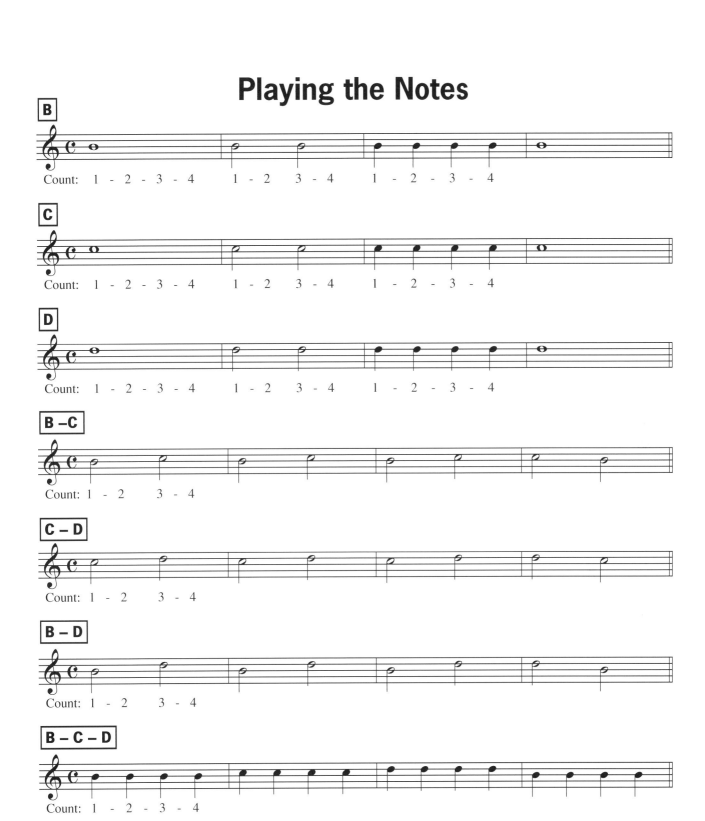

Playing on 2 Strings

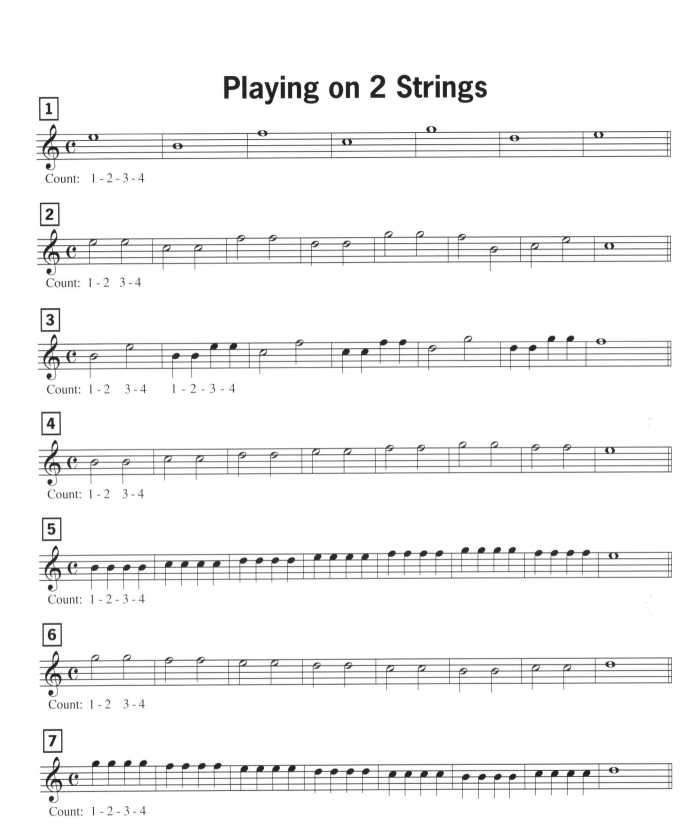

March

Steps

Study #1

Study #2

Three-Four Time

This sign indicates **three-four** time.

3 – beats per measure.
4 – type of note receiving one beat (quarter note).

In three-four time, we will have three beats per measure.

Dotted Half Notes

A dot (•) placed behind a note increases its value by one-half.

A dotted half note (𝅗𝅥•) will receive three beats.

Examples: 𝅗𝅥 = 2 counts   𝅗𝅥• = 3 counts

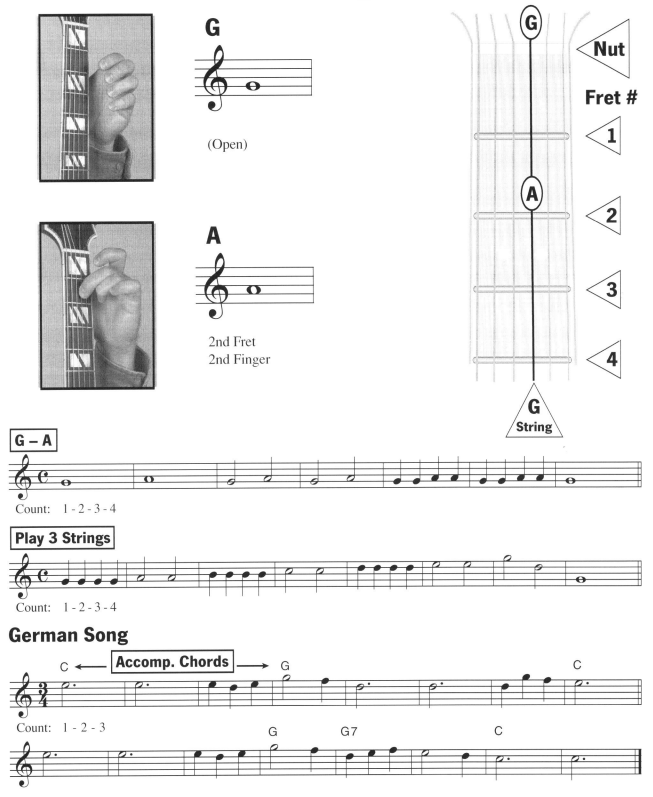

Rock Feeling

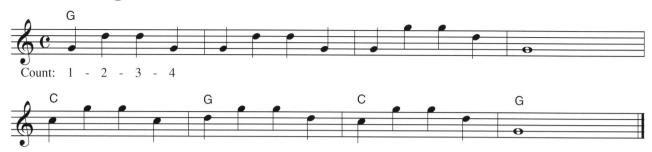

Indian Prayer

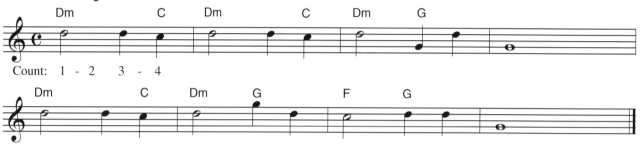

Good King Wenceslas

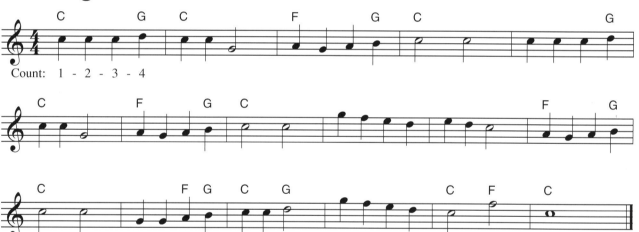

African Hymn

Prelude

Descending

Ascending

Sunset
Teacher Acc.

Aura Lee
Teacher Acc.   Folk Song

Pick-Up Notes

One or more notes at the beginning of a strain before the first measure are referred to as **pick-up notes**.

The rhythm for pick-up notes is taken from the last measure of the selection and the beats are counted as such.

When the Saints Go Marchin' In

Two Note Pick-up

One Note Pick-up

The Tie

The **tie** is a curved line between two notes of the same pitch. The first note is played and held for the time duration of both. The second note is not played, but held.

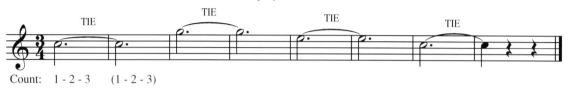

Psalm 100

Teacher Acc.

Louis Bourgeois
1510–1561

Red River Valley

Teacher Acc.

Western Song

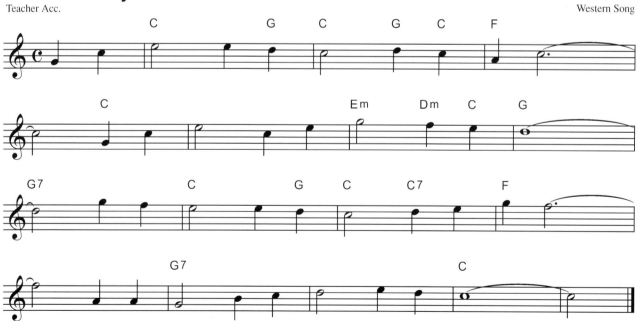

Notes on the D String

Fourth String

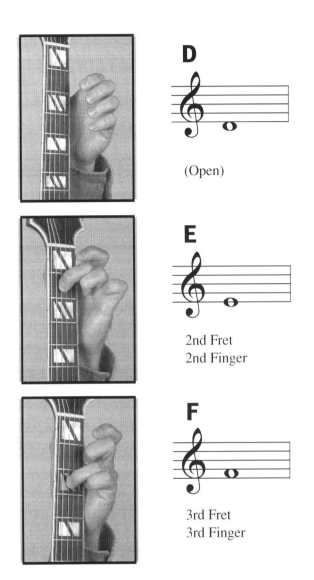

D

(Open)

E

2nd Fret
2nd Finger

F

3rd Fret
3rd Finger

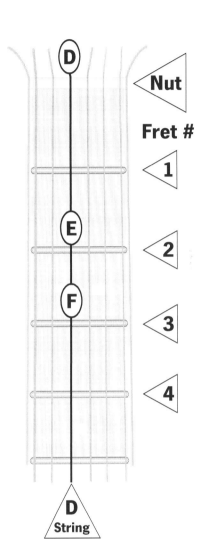

4 String Note Review

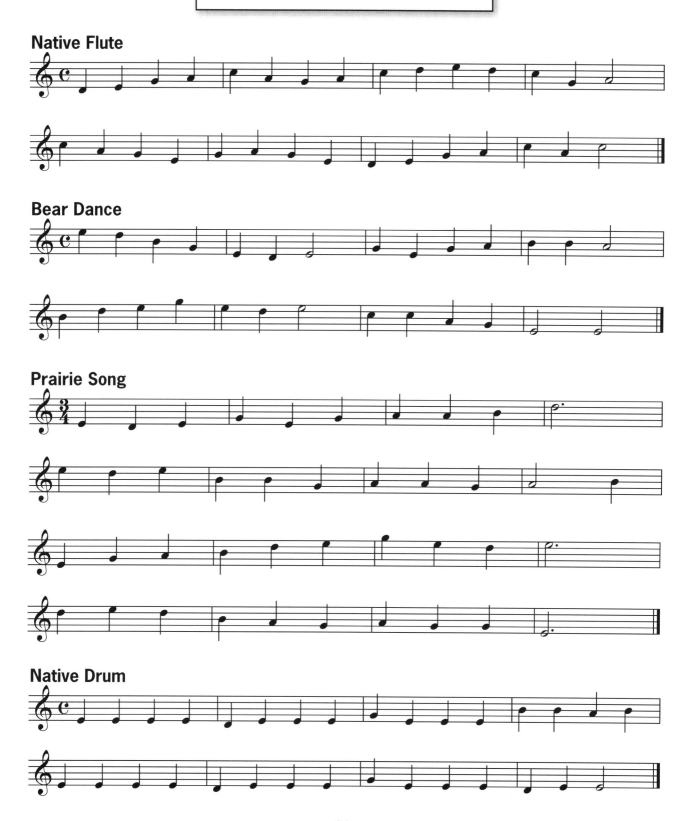

Cockles and Mussels
Teacher Acc.

Hymn
Teacher Acc.

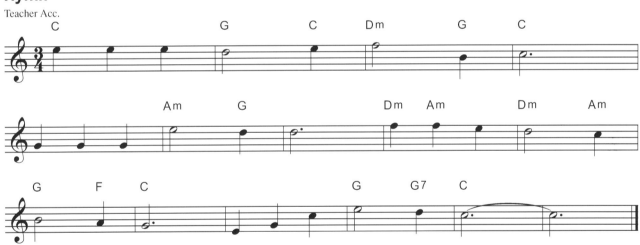

German Waltz
Teacher Acc.

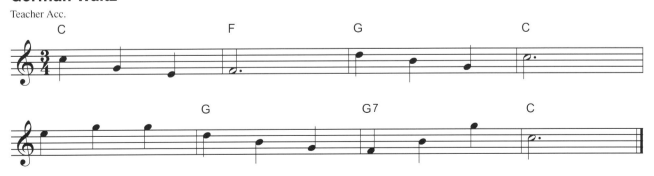

The Eighth Note

An **eighth note** receives one-half beat. (One quarter note equals two eighth notes.)

An eighth note will have a head, stem, and flag. If two or more are in successive order, they may be connected by a beam. (See example.)

Tudor Dance

Mohican Lament

Dance of the Royal Court

Village Waltz

Amazing Grace
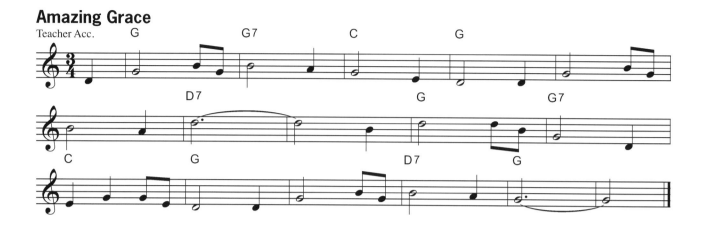

Tenting Tonight

Melancholy

The Slur/Hammer–on/Pull–off

A *slur* is a curved line that connects two or more notes of a different pitch. **When a slur occurs, pick only the first note.** The remaining notes are fingered but not picked. A slur going up in pitch is sometimes called a *hammer–on*. A slur going down in pitch is sometimes called a *pull–off*.

Blue Ridge

Celtic Dawn

Swamp Buggy

Morning Song

Acc. Chords

WB
Early American
Hymn Melody

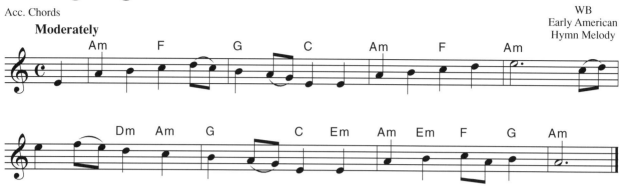

Repeat Sign

Repeat signs look like this: ||: :||

When they occur, repeat the music found between the signs.

Cripple Creek

Acc. Chords

WB
Western American
Gold Mining Song

Early Christmas Morn

WB
13th Century English

Acc. Chords

Solos

Spanish Nights
Acc. Chords
Medium tempo
WB

Four–String Blues
Acc. Chords
Easy walking tempo
WB

Irish Mist
WB
Bright

Dotted Quarter Notes

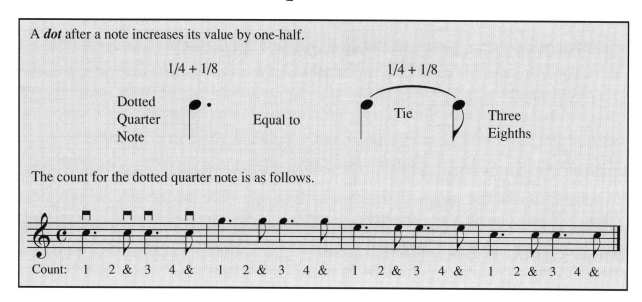

Our Boys Will Shine Tonight

The Roving Gambler

More Solos

This Little Light of Mine

Precious Memories

Early American Hymn

Come and Go with Me

Salty Dog Blues

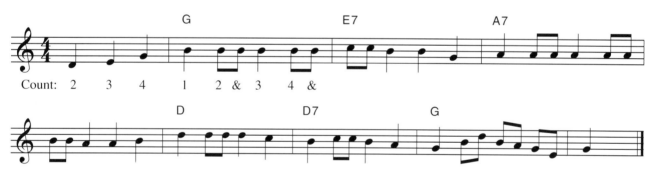

Steal Away

Notes on the A String

Fifth String

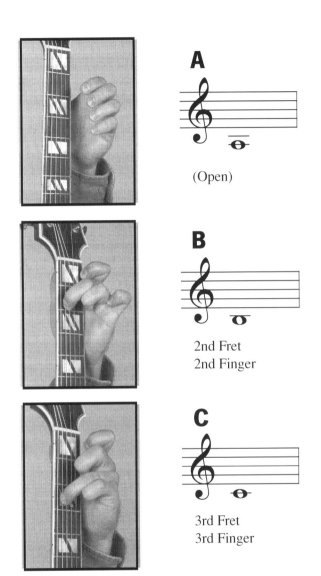

A

(Open)

B

2nd Fret
2nd Finger

C

3rd Fret
3rd Finger

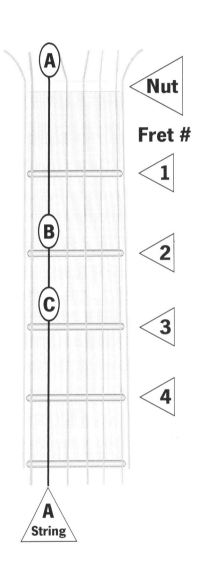

Low Gear

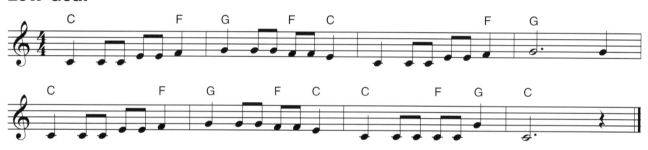

Volga Boatmen

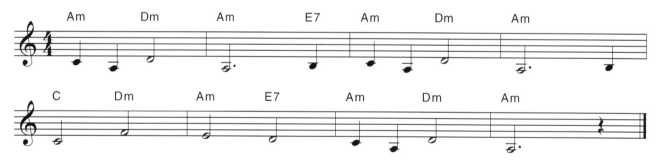

Power Drive

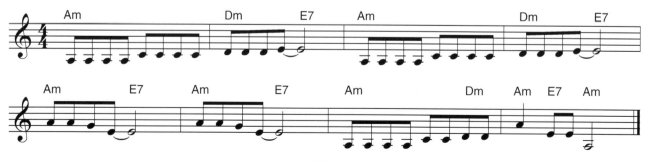

QUARTER NOTES

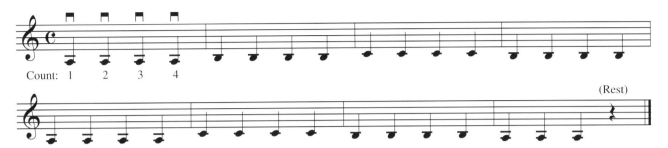

Wilderness Trail

Westward Ho!

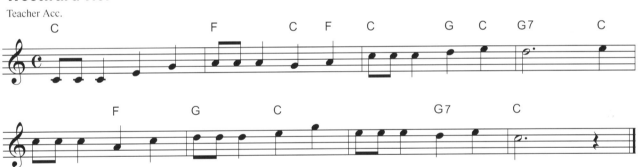

Chord Waltz

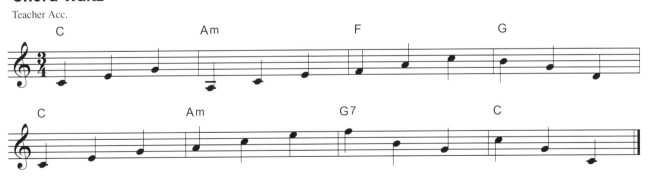

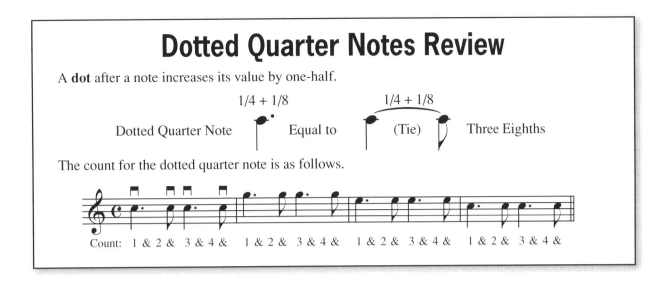

Kum-Ba-Ya
Teacher Acc.
African Hymn

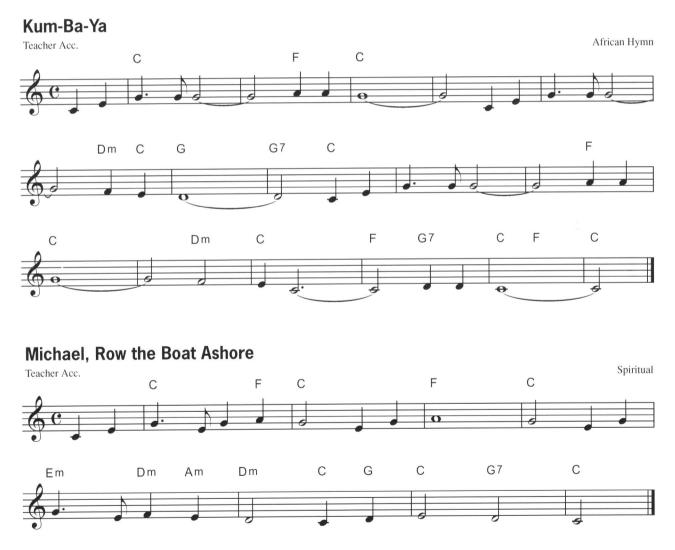

Michael, Row the Boat Ashore
Teacher Acc.
Spiritual

Mountain Flower
Teacher Acc.

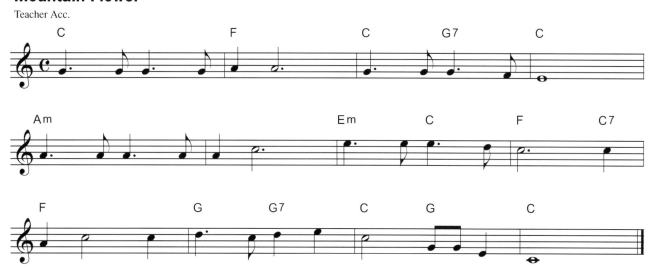

Quest
Teacher Acc.

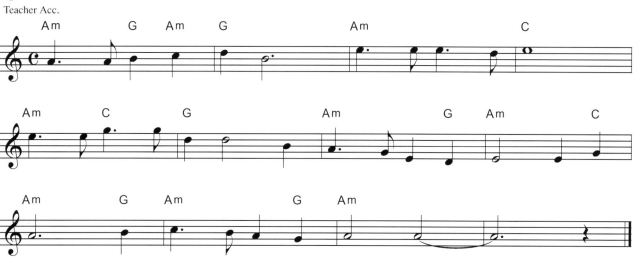

Homeward Bound
Teacher Acc.

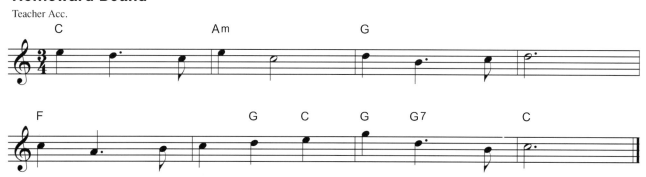

Note Review

Daydreams

Ozark Stream

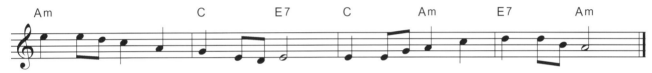

Waterfall

Mountain Trail

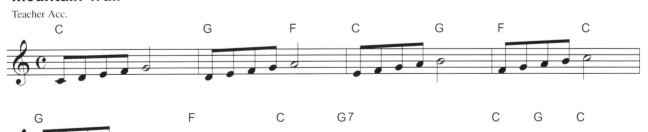

Notes on the Low E String

Sixth String

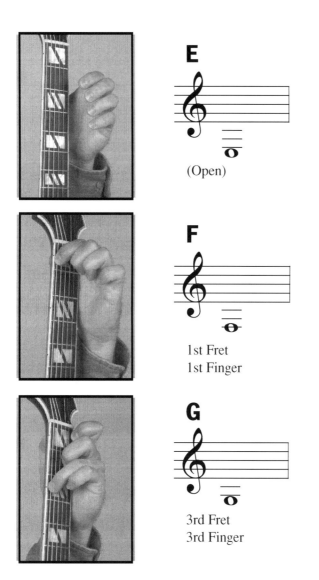

E
(Open)

F
1st Fret
1st Finger

G
3rd Fret
3rd Finger

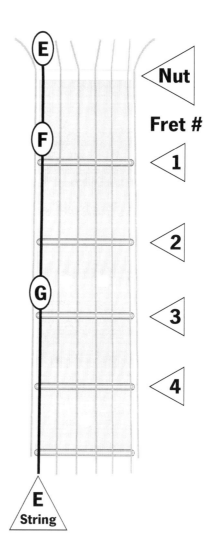

Driving Bass
Teacher Acc.

Low Gear
Teacher Acc.

Running the Notes
Teacher Acc.

The Clock
Acc. Chords
Moderately

Echoes
Acc. Chords
Smoothly

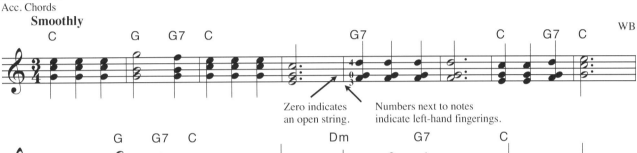

Zero indicates an open string.
Numbers next to notes indicate left-hand fingerings.

Arpeggio Picking
Acc. Chords
Flowing

Chimes
Acc. Chords
Medium, Gently

Playing High A

Smoky Ridge
Teacher Acc.

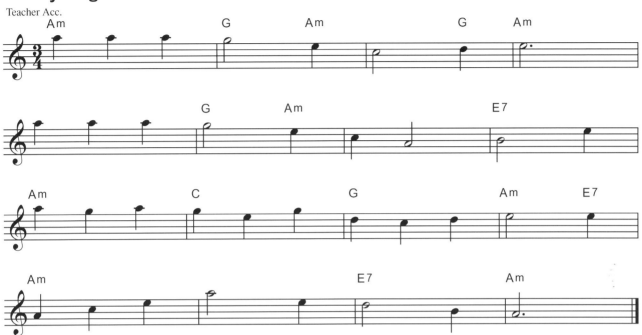

Voyage
Teacher Acc.

Chords

A **melody** is a succession of single tones.

A **chord** is a combination of three or more tones sounded together.

Tones in a Melody

The Same Tones as a Chord

We will construct our chords by playing the chordal tones separately as in a melody and, without raising the fingers, striking them together.

The Chord Waltz

The Builder

Small Chord Etude

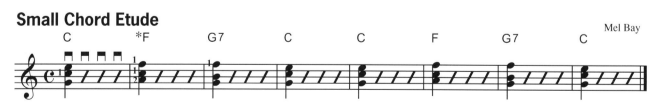

Practice the above etude until it can be played without missing a beat.

*Note that the first finger holds down two notes (C-F) in the second chord.

/ = Strum chord down across strings.

First and Second Endings

Sometimes in a song a first and second ending appear. When this occurs, take the first ending and observe the repeat sign. Then, on the second time through, skip the first ending, play the second ending, and continue on with the music. (Sometimes the song will end with the second ending.)

Hungarian Dance #4

The Sally Gardens

Building the F Chord

Two Notes

Three Notes

Four Notes

Four-String Chord Study

We use the same method for building four-string chords as we did in building three-string chords. Play the chordal tones melodically, holding the fingers down until the full chord is reached, then strike the strings together producing the desired chord.

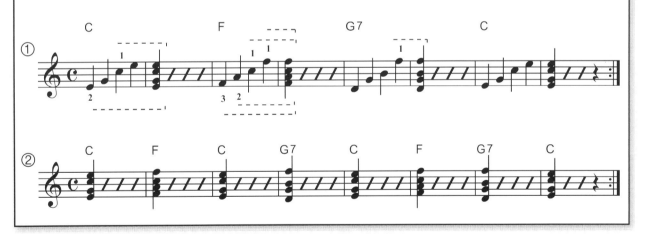

Chimes

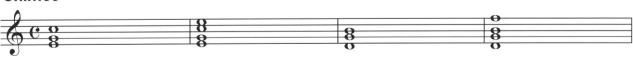

My Country Tis of Thee
Teacher Acc.

Green Grow the Lilacs
Teacher Acc.

Chord Bouquet
Teacher Acc.

Bass Solos with Chord Accompaniment

When playing bass solos with chord accompaniment, you will find the solo with the stems turned downward and the accompaniment with the stems turned upward.

In the example shown above, you see the dotted half note (E) with the stem downward. It is played on the count of one and held for counts two and three.

The quarter rest over the dotted half note indicates that there is no chord accompanimet at the count of one. The chords with the stems upward are played on counts two and three.

Gliding Along

Mel Bay

Hymn
Teacher Acc.

Country Waltz
Teacher Acc.

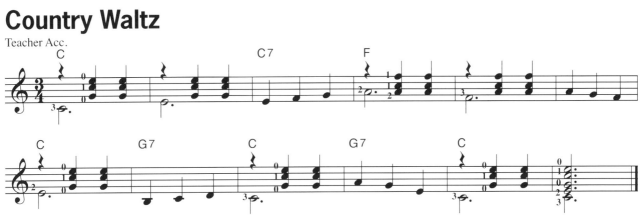

Western Song
Teacher Acc.

Oh Bury Me Not on the Lone Prairie
Teacher Acc.

Red River Valley
Teacher Acc.

Sawdust Trail
Teacher Acc.

The Key of C

In the C scale the first note is a C and we proceed through the musical alphabet until C reappears: C-D-E-F-G-A-B-C.

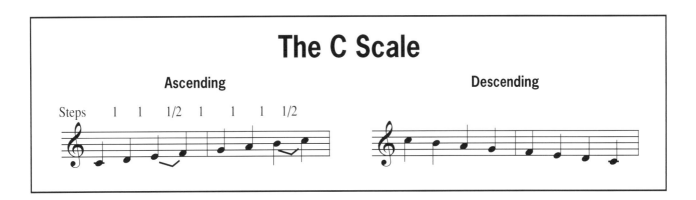

Scale Studies

C Velocity Study #1
C Velocity Study #2
C Velocity Study #3
C Velocity Study #4

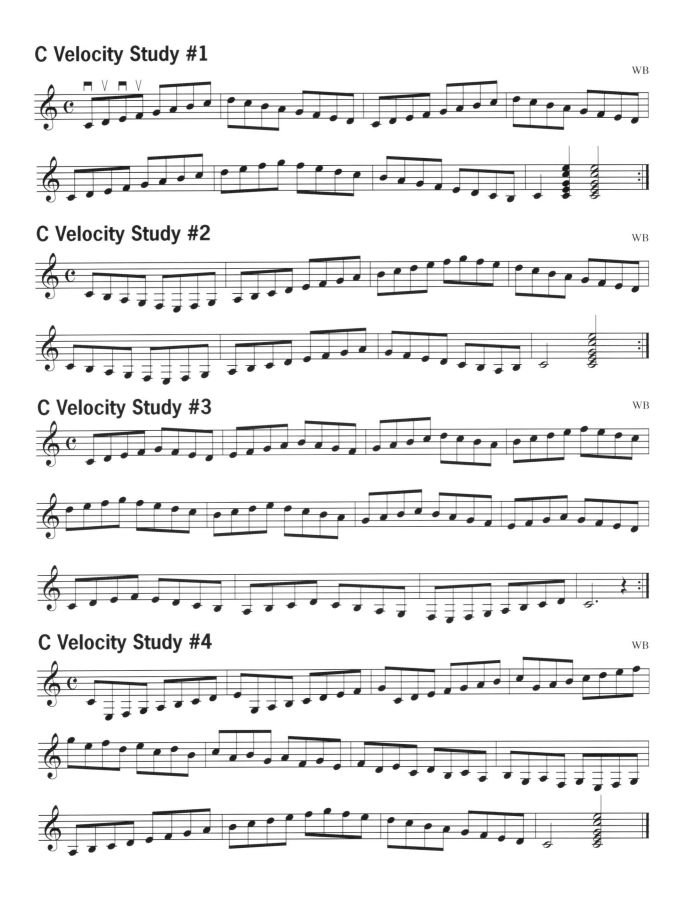

Solos

Blow, Ye Winds
Acc. Chords
WB
Sea Chanty
Brightly

Early American Hymn
Acc. Chords
WB
Slowly

Bass Line Lead/Bluegrass Style
Acc. Chords
WB
Swing feeling

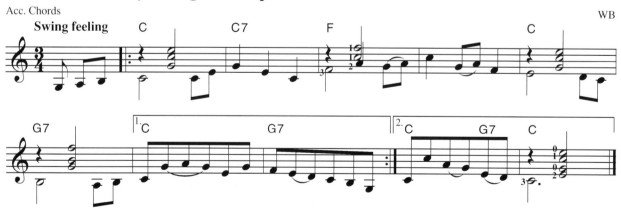

Shenandoah

Teacher Acc.

Shenandoah – Advanced Version

Teacher Acc.

Blue Bells of Scotland
Teacher Acc.

Blue Bells of Scotland – Advanced Version
Teacher Acc.

Chords in the Key of C Major

The key of C has three principal chords. They are C, F, and G7.

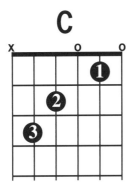
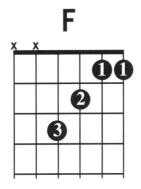
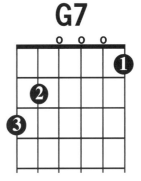

- The circles indicate the position where your fingers should be placed.
- Numerals inside circles indicate the fingers.
- "X" over the strings means that the strings are not to be played.
- "O" over the strings indicates the strings be played open.
- Place fingers in positions indicated by the circles and strike them all together.

Musical Notation of the Chords

Accompaniment Styles

Alternate Basses

In Three-Four Time

Chord Studies in C

Home, Home, Can I Forget Thee

Long, Long Ago

Steps

A half-step is the distance from a given tone to the next higher or lower tone. On the guitar, the distance of a half step is one fret.

A whole step consists of two half steps, The distance of a whole step on the guitar is two frets.

The C scale has two half steps. They are between E-F and B-C. Note the distance of one fret between those notes. The distances between C-D, D-E, F-G, G-A, and A-B are whole steps.

Whole steps and half steps are also referred to as whole tones and half tones, We will refer to them as whole steps and half steps.

Chromatics

The alteration of the pitches of tones is brought about by the use of symbols called **chromatics** (also) referred to as **accidentals**).

The Sharp ♯

The sharp placed before a note raises its pitch 1/2 step or one fret.

The Flat ♭

The flat placed before a note lowers its pitch 1/2 step or one fret.

The Natural ♮

The natural restores a note to its normal position. It cancels all accidentas previously used.

Sharps

A **sharp** placed in front of a note *raises* the pitch 1/2 step or one fret. Study the notes below

1st String

Remember: when a note is sharped, all notes of that pitch remain sharped throughout the measure unless a **natural sign** (♮) appears. A natural sign cancels a sharp.

1st String Sharps & Naturals

2nd String

3rd String

4th String

5th String

6th String

Walking Guitar

Flats

A **flat** (♭) placed in front of a note lowers the pitch 1/2 step or one fret. Study the notes below.
A **natural sign** (♮) cancels out the flat.

1st String

2nd String

3rd String

4th String

5th String

6th String

Benny's Flat

Alternate Picking

One of the most difficult things for the student is the mastery of the alternate stroke on diatonic passages.

To promote greater speed with proper accentation, the alternate stroke should be developed.

The following study will seem difficult at first; but, by practicing slowly and placing the downstrokes on the beats followed by an upstroke, the desired result will be accomplished.

Key of C Review

Etude

Count: 1 & 2 & 3 & 4 &

Picking Studies

①

②

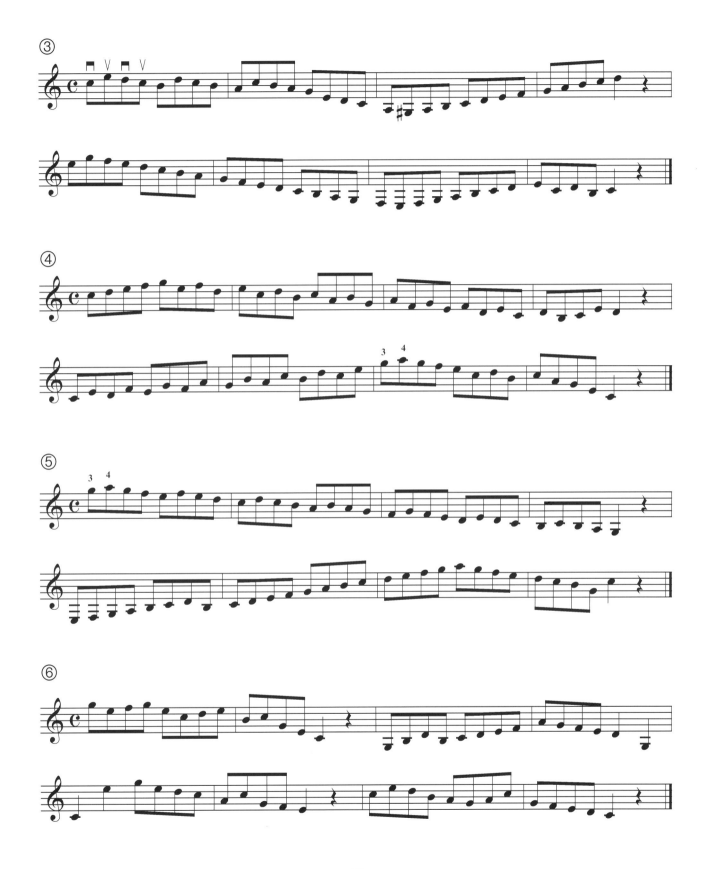

A Daily Scale Study

Count: 1 & 2 & 3 & 4 &

(Repeat ⊓ V ⊓ V)

The above study should be played sowly with a gradual increase of speed until a moderate tempo has been reached. It is an excellent daily exercise.

Running Around

Teacher Acc.

Key Signature

When a sharp appears in the key signature, all notes of that pitch are sharped unless cancelled by a natural sign (♮).

Can Can

Polovetsian Dance

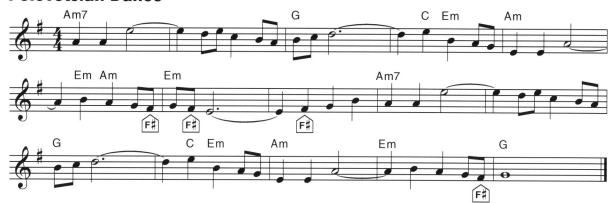

Hey, Ho, Nobody's Home

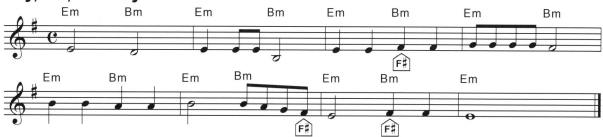

Eighth Rest (𝄾)

Receives the same time value as an eighth note.

I'm Gonna Play

More Solos

Remember — if F♯ is in the key signature, all F's will be sharped unless a natural sign (♮) is in front of the F.

Matty Groves

Minuet by Bach

Waltzing Matilda

Repeat Signs Review

Means to go back and repeat the phrase.

Forest Green

Red Wing

Once in David's Royal City

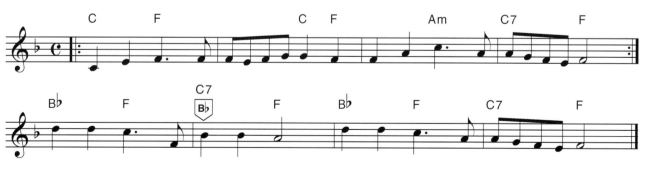

More Solos

Watch the key signature for B♭s!

Waltz by Chopin

Ding, Dong, Merrily on High

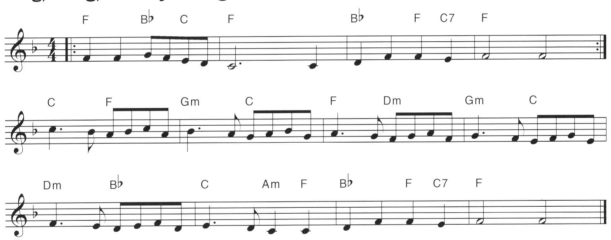

Traumerai by Schumann

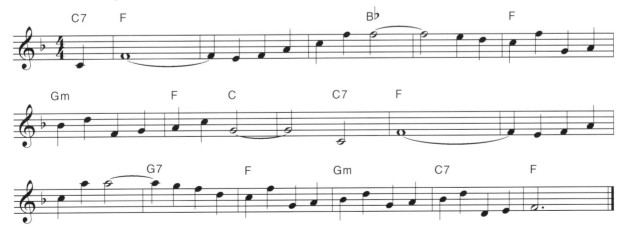

Bull Durham

D.C. al Fine means to go back to the beginning of the piece and play until you see the word "fine" which means "the end." The repeats are not usually taken on the D.C.

Frolic

Frog Junction

W. Bay

Swing Feeling

Catawissa Blues

W. Bay

Slowly

The Key of A Minor

(Relative to C Major)

- Each major key will have a relative minor key.
- The relative minor scale is built upon the sixth tone of the major scale.
- The key signature of both will be the same.
- The minor scale will have the same number of tones (7) as the major.
- The difference between the two scales is the arrangement of the whole steps and half steps.
- There are three forms of the minor scale: 1) pure or natural, 2) harmonic, 3) melodic.

The A Minor Scale

Natural (Pure)

Harmonic

The 7th tone is raised one half step ascending and descending.

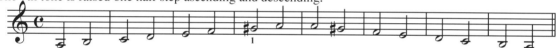

Melodic

The 6th and 7th tones are raised one half step ascending and lowered back to their normal pitch descending.

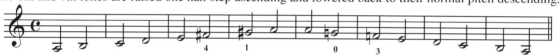

The Chords in the Key of A Minor

m = minor

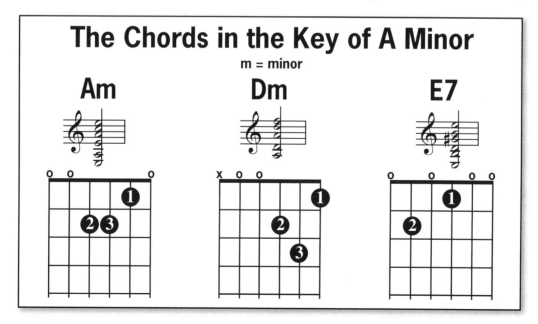

84

Accompaniment Styles in A Minor

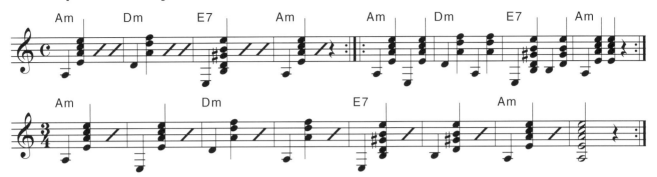

Orchestration Style

The Diagonal line (/) indicates a chord stroke. They will fall only on each beat of the measure.

Repeat the accompaniment exercises until they can be played without missing a beat.

Chord Studies in the Key of Am

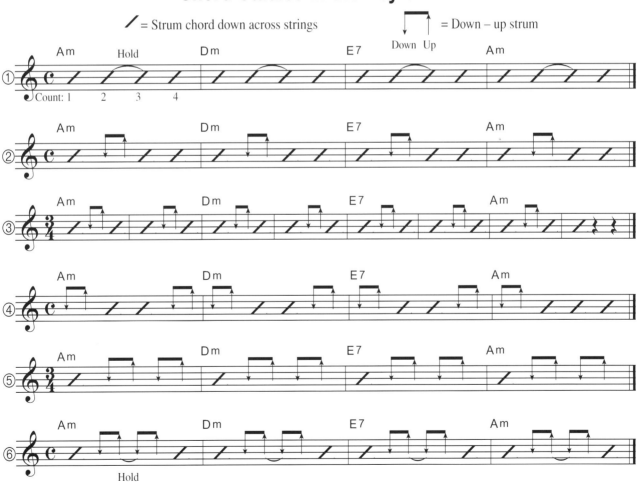

Key of A minor
The Natural A Minor Scale

You will notice that, like the C scale, there are no sharps or flats.

Velocity Study

A Harmonic Minor

In a harmonic minor scale the 7th tone of the scale is sharped. Thus with the "A" Harmonic Minor, all G's are played as G♯.

Velocity Study

A Daily Scale Study in A Minor
Harmonic

(Repeat ⊓∨⊓∨)

Picking Studies in A Minor
①

②

③

Sailing
Teacher Acc.

Minor Song
Teacher Acc.

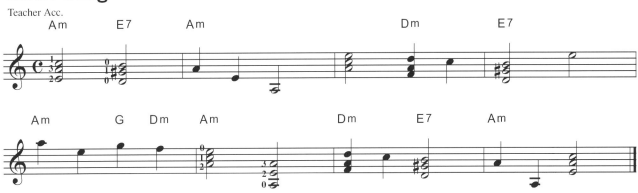

Journey
Teacher Acc.

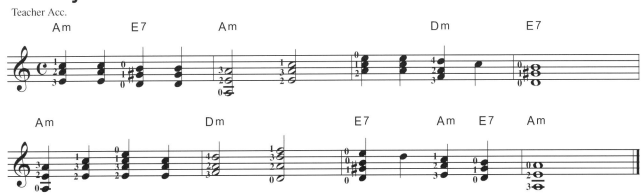

Hold Sign: 𝄐 This sign placed over or under a note or rest indicates the prolonging of its time value.

Wayfaring Stranger

Another Daily Scale Study in A Minor

(Repeat ⊓ V ⊓ V)

The Up Stroke: V   This stroke will be used on repeated eighth notes of the same pitch.

A Visit to the Relatives

Sakura

Slowly

Minuet

Acc. Chords
Briskly

WB
Henry Purcell

D.S. 𝄋 al Fine

When this phrase appears at the end of a piece (**D.S. 𝄋 *al Fine***) go back to the sign (𝄋) and play until you see the word **"Fine,"** which means "The End."

Menuet

Acc. Chords

WB
Johann Quantz

92

Caleb's Gorge
Acc. Chords

Parson's Farewell
Acc. Chords

English Country Dance
By John Playford 1651

Eleven Mile Canyon

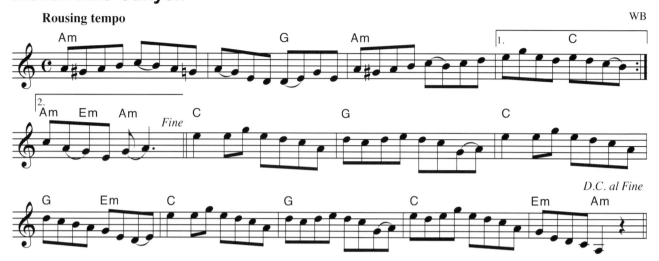

Star of the County Down

Anitra's Dance Theme

Arcadian Melody

Picking Solos

Foggy Mountain Run
Teacher Acc.

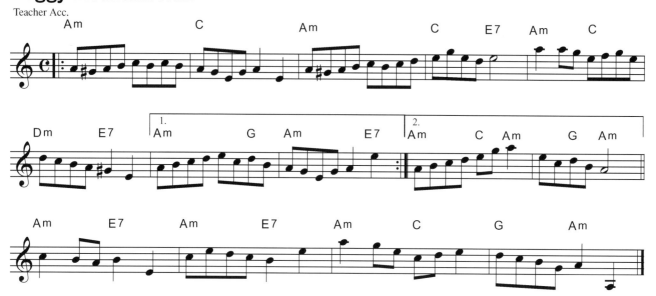

The Shire
Teacher Acc.

Bluegrass Sunrise
Teacher Acc.

Cradle Song
Teacher Acc.

Blue Ridge Trail
Teacher Acc.

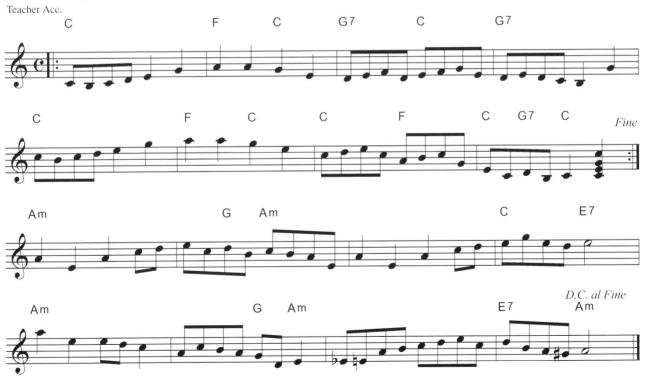

Lafayette Square

Shady Grove

Key of A Minor Review

Picking Studies

Prelude in C/Am

Slowy

W. Bay

C/Am Etude

Moderately

W. Bay

Valse

Flowing Tempo

W. Bay

Russian Dance

Allegro

W. Bay

The Key of G

The key of G will have one sharp (F#). It will be identified by this signature:

The F notes will be played as shown:

6th String	4th String	1st String
2nd Fret	4th Fret	2nd Fret
2nd Finger.	4th Finger.	2nd Finger.

The G Scale

Note that, in order to have the half steps falling between the seventh and eighth degrees of the scale, the F must be sharped. Our major scale pattern is then correct (1-1-1/2-1-1-1-1/2 Steps).

A Daily Drill

Picking Studies in G

①

G Scale Velocity Study #1

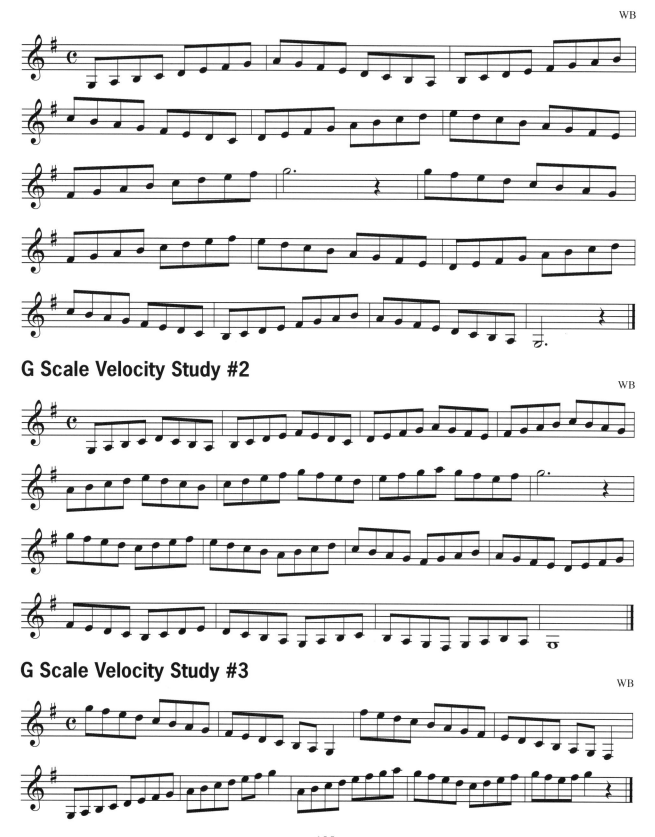

G Scale Velocity Study #2

G Scale Velocity Study #3

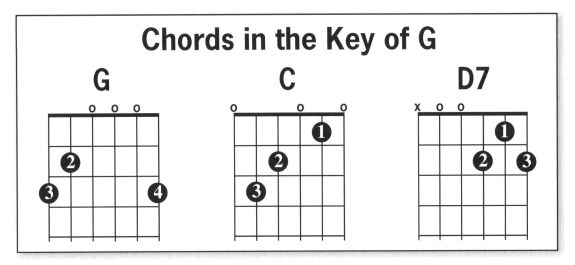

Accompaniment Styles in the Key of G

G Boogie
Teacher Acc.

In the Evening by the Moonlight

 The following etude introduces the notes D and B being played together. This is done by playing the note D with the first finger on the third fret of the second string and playing the note B with the second finger on the fourth fret of the **third string**.

Etude

Far From Home

Flatpick Solo or Acc. Chords

Lively tempo

WB
Shetland Island Reel

On the Banks of that Lonely River

Flatpick Solo or Acc. Chords

Slowly, with feeling

WB
Southern Mountain Ballad

Slane

Flatpick Solo or Acc. Chords

WB
Irish Hymn

Bransle Double

Flatpick Solo or Acc. Chords

WB
Michael Praetorius

Ballad
Flatpick Solo

Rondeau
Flatpick Solo or Acc. Chords

Gavotte
Flatpick Solo

Two-Four Time

This sign  indicates **two-four** time.

2 – beats per measure.
4 – a quarter note receives one beat.

Two-four time will have two beats per measure with the quarter note receiving one beat.

The Old Mill
Guitar Duet

Two-Four Picking
Teacher Acc.

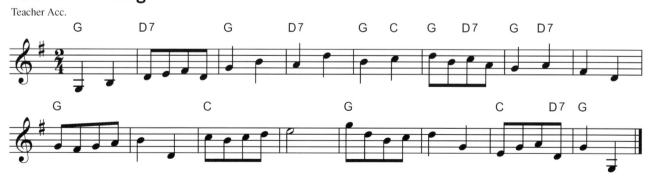

The Little Prince
Guitar Duet

Mazas
Arr. by Mel Bay

Carry Me Back to Old Virginny
Guitar Solo

Bland
Arr. by Mel Bay

* The wavy line before the last chord means to glide the pick slowly over the strings, producing a harp-like effect. The musical term for this is **Quasi Arpi**.

Grace Notes

A *grace note* is a tiny note that appears before another note. There may be one or more grace notes. They are connected by a slur to the note they precede. Grace notes "borrow" their time value from the main note. Grace notes call for a quick hammer–on, pull–off, or combination of both. Grace notes are prevalent in Baroque music but also in Celtic, country, and bluegrass!

Grace Note Studies

The Flowers of Sweet Erin the Green

Flatpick Solo or Acc. Chords

WB
Celtic Ballad

*Slide Review

The above solo used a slide. Remember, a slide is shown by a slanted line leading into a note. To play a slide, finger the note *two frets* below the desired note. Then, without lifting your finger, slide up to the correct pitch.

Key of G Review

Picking Studies

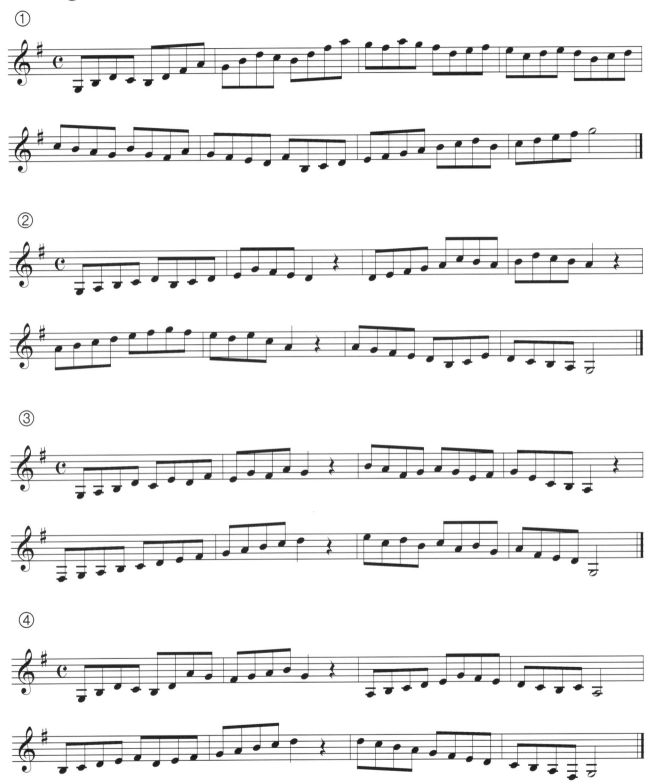

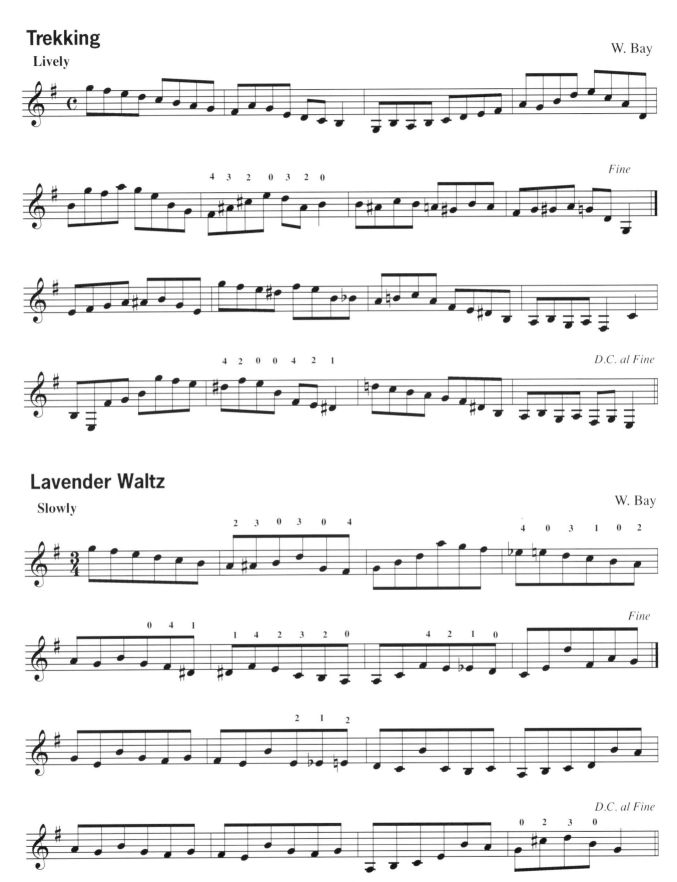

Accidentals are effective only in the measures in which they are found. When that measure is passed, the accidentals become void.

In the following solo, *The Guachos*, the third part is in the key of C, which explains the natural on the fifth line in the signature.

The Gauchos
Guitar Solo

Carcassi - Bay

Poinsietta

Freely

W. Bay

The Key of E Minor

(Relative to G Major)

The key of E minor will have the same key signature as G major.

Two E Minor Scales

Harmonic

Melodic

The above scales should be memorized.

Picking Studies

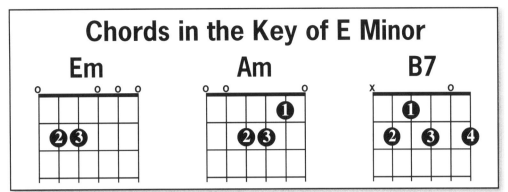

Accompaniment Styles in the Key of E Minor

* This sign (∤) means that the previous measure is to be repeated.

Orchestration Styles

Chord Studies

East River

Goblins

Chord Review

- The key of C has six chords. They are C, F, G7, Am, Dm, and E7.
- The latter three are in the relative minor key but use the key signature of C.
- All "outside" chords are **Accidental Chords**.
- The most commonly used of these chords are D7 and A7.
- The six chords found in the key of G are G, C, D7, Em, Am, and B7.
- The most common accidental chords found in the key of G are A7 and E7.

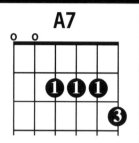

Spotting the accidentals in the various chords will facilitate the reading of them... for example:
- B7 will have a D♯
- E7 will have a G♯
- A7 will have a C♯
- D7 will have a F♯

In the following studies, you will see how they appear.

Lament

Guitar Solo

Mel Bay

Night Voyage

Buena Vista

Flatpick Solo

Shabat Shalom
(Song for the Sabbath)

Flatpick Solo

Shaker Dance

Flatpick Solo

Johnny Has Gone For A Soldier

In this beautiful ballad we have a fermata (𝄐). When this sign occurs hold the note or notes under the sign for an extended period of time.

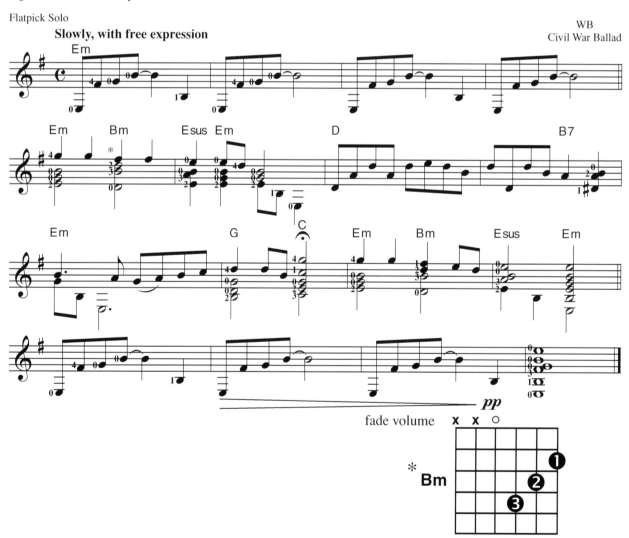

The Clergy's Lamentation

Flatpick Solo

WB
Turlough O'Carolan

Tambourin

Flatpick Solo

WB
Rameau

E Minor Review

Picking Studies

Excursion

Andante   W. Bay

Jazz Etude

Swing Feeling   W. Bay

Wade in the Water

Moderately Spiritual

Coldwater Creek

Swing Feeling W. Bay

Musical Terms
Tempo Terms

Largo	Very Slowly
Lento	Slowly
Adagio	Slowly with a very expressive feeling
Andante	A walking speed, however not too fast
Moderato	Moderately, medium speed
Allegretto	Slightly more movement than Moderato
Allegro	Quickly, lively tempo, but not overly fast or "out of control"
Vivaci	Very fast
Rit. "Ritardando"	Slow down at a gradual rate
Acc. "Accelerando"	Accelerate or speed up at a gradual rate

Dynamics

pp	(pianissimo)	Very soft
p	(piano)	Soft
mp	(mezzo piano)	Medium soft
mf	(mezzo forte)	Medium loud
f	(forte)	Loud
ff	(fortissimo)	Very loud
$<$	(crescendo)	Gradually get louder
$>$	(decresendo)	Gradually get softer
>	(accent)	The note is to be played louder

Phrasing Terms

8va	Play the passage 8 notes or one octave higher
Staccato	Play the notes so marked in a short detached manner
Legato	Play the notes or pluck the note in a gentle somewhat connected manner. Almost as if the notes are slurred.
Rubato	Very expressive, no set tempo; notes may be played longer or shorter than their exact value in order to add expression.
ad lib	Playing at liberty, playing in a totally free fashion; improvising or making up a melody if a given section is marked so in a piece.

Made in the USA
Middletown, DE
21 July 2015